Stories F
The

Stagger
Inn

K M Murphy

For all the regulars in their local pubs.

Acknowledgements

To my husband, thank you for your continued support and for being so awesome!

Disclaimer :-

This is a work of fiction. Names, characteristics, businesses, places, events and incidents are either a product of the imagination or used in a fictitious manner. Any resemblance to actual persons, living or dead, or actual events are purely coincidental.

Contents :-

Introduction

The small village local pub. I've found that there's nowhere else quite like it.

It has a warm familiarity to it, kinda homely, where you instantly feel at ease when you walk through the door.

A place where the regulars congregate to enjoy each other's company or more often than not, to wind each other up!

It's like a cross between a second family and a playground for adults!

Working behind the bar of such a place, I experienced the on goings in the pub from a very different perspective, most likely because I was the only sober person in the room.

At 29-years-old, I was often the youngest person in the pub. But I enjoyed being in the company of an older generation, I admired their resilience and depth of character.

So, I started each shift with a smile anticipating which punters would be in each day and what antics they would get up to.

Having got to know all the regulars in the pub well, I still could never predict how each shift would go. I've never known a place like it where such random and hilarious incidents occur.

It's also a place where I've witnessed and been part of some of the most fascinating conversations and amazing stories I've ever heard.

I hope you enjoy reading these stories from the Stagger Inn as much as I did being a part of them.

8

Anyone for Doms?

Off I went to start my shift at the pub, it was a nice warm summers afternoon so I decided to leave the car and walk. The pub was only about half a mile away from my house, so it wouldn't take me long to walk there.

So, I grabbed a coat for the return journey and headed out the front door.

The pub was situated at the far end of the village and the easiest route was straight along the main street.

As I was walking along, I passed the butchers shop and Bert stuck his head out of the door and said, "Is that you away to open up Kirsty?"

I said, "Aye, Bert. I'm away to get started."

Bert said, "My Irene's just sent me up tae get stew for tomorrows steak pie. Once I've dropped this stew in tae Irene, I'll stop in and get Rusty then we'll be in later."

I said, "Nae bother, Bert, I'll see you in a bit," and I continued on my way to the pub.

Bert was one of the regulars in the pub, he was in most days for a few hours, usually with his best pal Rusty. Bert was a great guy, I think he was about 75-years-old. He had such a pleasant, decent way about him. He never had a bad word to say about anyone and had time for everyone.

He didn't particularly have any distinguishing features about him. He was of average height and build and I suppose looked like the stereotypical image of your average grandad. He usually wore trousers and a polo shirt and often a body warmer or tank top.

I enjoyed being in Bert's company and was glad when he said that he and Rusty would be in the pub later.

As I approached the pub I observed how the old stonework of the building still looked so solid. The building was well over one-hundred years old, I think the pub and the church were the oldest buildings in the village.

The Stagger Inn still had an old fashioned wooden exterior door with huge black iron hinges. It had its original lock on the door but had been updated with a more modern style of lock and had extra bolts fitted to make it more secure.

I put the key in the door, slid back the bolts and opened the door. When I walked in there was a faint smell of beer and when I looked around I saw that there were still a few pints sitting on a table from the night before. So, I left the front door open to let the fresh air in and cleared away the left-over pints and wiped the wooden tables down.

It wasn't long before my first customers were through the door and the pub was starting to fill up. A Thursday was usually a busy day, I was expecting the usual punters in the afternoon then would wait and see what the evening brought.

It was about 4 pm when Bert and Rusty walked through the door. Bert shouted, "Hiya Kirsty, hen," as he and Rusty walked towards the bar.

Rusty said, "We got you tonight then Kirsty have we?"

I said, "You sure have Rusty, all night too."

Then I said to Bert, "I thought you'd be at home making that steak pie for tomorrows dinner?"

Bert laughed and said, "Oh naw, that's Irene's department, I just like eating it."

I said, "So is it the usual then?"

They both said aye and Rusty went and sat at their table. I often wondered what would happen if someone else sat at Bert and Rusty's table, but no-one ever did.

I reached under the bar and retrieved Bert's whiskey tumbler, he had a specific tumbler that he took his whiskey in. His daughter had given him it as a Christmas present and he brought it to the pub one day and has been drinking out of it ever since. Bert said that it was the perfect tumbler for measuring how much water he took in his whiskey. There was a gold image of a stag's head on the tumbler and Bert said that once his whiskey measure was in the tumbler, water was to be poured in until it reached the top of the stags' antlers. According to Bert, that was the perfect half.

I poured Bert's perfect half, a half of 'Bells' whiskey for Rusty with one cube of ice in it, a half-pint of lager for Rusty and a half-pint of heavy for Bert.

I said, "You wanting me to bring it over for you?"

Bert said, "Naw hen, it's alright, I've got it."

I watched Bert as he walked with his tray of drinks, being careful not to spill anything and sat beside Rusty at their table. They looked so content together, you could tell that they had been friends for a long time and were used to each other's company.

I never knew what Rusty's real name was, he was called Rusty because he used to have bright ginger hair when he was younger but it was grey and thinned now.

The pub filled up quickly on this particular shift and by about 6 pm almost all the tables were full.

I noticed that a fair few of the regulars were in, Jim, Cammy, Ian, Pete, Alec, Jock, Sleepy Joe, Watty and Shug.

There were loads of conversations going on, folk going outside to have cigarettes or a smoke of their pipe, some were playing dominoes at a table and others generally mingling about and having a laugh.

I was kept quite busy between serving at the bar, clearing the tables and washing glasses. Even when I was busy I still felt entertained by the punters and it was usually by how they spoke to each other. They

11

always had great banter with each other. I regularly found myself laughing away at the things I would overhear.

Some of my favourite phrases were, "Away and no talk shite", "Your patters pish man", "Gies peace ya fucking eejit" and "Away and chase yersel."

My own dad used to tell me and brother's to, 'away and chase yersel,' when we were little and I often thought, how on earth are you supposed to chase yourself?

I have never again in my life encountered a group of men who could cut each other to the bone with their insults but still be best of friends and no offence taken. These guys were certainly not precious but at the same time were also kind, decent and had a great sense of right from wrong.

I noticed that Jim had joined Bert and Rusty at their table and they had started to play a game of dominoes and were quite happily playing away.

On the other side of the pub, I could hear that Pete was getting rather loud. He was one of those kinda guys that you were just aware of when he was around, I imagined he would be the life and soul of a party, always laughing and joking and loud with it. So, to notice that he was getting loud meant that he was really loud and probably starting to annoy folk. He never sat in the same seat or stood in the same place for long, he went around all the tables and mixed with all the different companies.

He was tall and slim, quite a wiry guy with plenty of energy. I always got on fine with him but I could see how he would get on some folk's nerves.

Bert tolerated Pete but Rusty couldn't be bothered with him, I'd heard Rusty describe Pete before as, "A glaikit eejit of a man."

It wasn't long before Pete made his way around the pub to Bert and Rusty's table and wanted to join the game of dominoes. I could see Rusty scowling and rolling his eyes at Pete but they let him join. It now became the loudest game of dominoes I've ever heard with Pete's constant commentary on ever turn and prediction of who would play which domino next. He kept winding the others up by saying they were cheating, dropping his dominoes on the floor or pinging his dominoes across the table into the game.

A few times I walked past when I was collecting glasses and I heard Rusty say to Pete, "Settle doon man, you're spoiling the game."

Pete just laughed and said, "Aw, I'm just having a laugh, ye nae sense of humour?"

Their game continued and I was serving Cammy at the bar when Rusty jumped out of his seat and shouted, "For fuck sake!"

Cammy and I both looked over at Rusty, surprised at his outburst. The rest of the pub had also heard him and quietened down to see what had happened.

Then Rusty started ranting, "See you, Pete, you did that deliberate. I telt you to settle doon, you're always acting like a fucking idiot and noo look what you've done!"

Rusty was going mental, I'd never seen him like that before. He was on his feet, leaning over the table pointing in Pete's face. I couldn't think what Pete could have done to have angered him so much.

Rusty then grabbed a handful of dominoes off the table and started flinging them at Pete, shouting, "Stupid arse that you are!"

Pete was shouting, "Whoa, whoa!" as he tried to dodge the flying dominoes.

I rushed over to their table and I put my hand on Rusty's arm and tried to lighten the situation by saying, "Deary me what's going on boys?"

Rusty sat back down in his chair and I noticed that there were dominoes all over the table, spilt drink and broken glass. Then I saw it and I thought, aw naw. Bert's special tumbler was lying smashed on the table.

Pete, while having a carry on, pinged a domino across the table and smashed it straight into Bert's stag tumbler.

Bert was trying to calm Rusty down by saying, "Come on Rusty, he didny mean it, it was an accident."

Bert being so understanding and forgiving seemed to rile Rusty even more.

Rusty shouted, "That's no the point though!"

Pete tried to apologise to Bert while Jim and I looked on. Pete even said that he'd buy Bert a new tumbler.

Then Rusty shouted, "It's no just any old tumbler, his lassie bought him that for his Christmas ye ken."

Pete then looked very awkward and said, "Aw, I'm sorry Bert."

I started to clean the broken glass and spilt drink from their table and I asked Pete to get me the broken glass bucket from behind the bar, to diffuse the situation and get Pete away from Rusty.

Everyone else in the bar went back about their business and Rusty seemed to settle down.

When I went back behind the bar I looked at the pieces of broken glass that were once Bert's favourite tumbler. I thought, what a shame, there was no saving it, it was smashed to smithereens.

Pete took himself over to the other side of the pub and put his jacket on, I thought maybe best he's decided to just go home. He had a defeated look about him and I did feel a bit sorry for him.

Pete said goodbye to a few people then he went back over to Bert and Rusty's table on his way out of the pub. I heard Pete apologising again to Bert then he said, "Oh here Rusty, I've got something for you," and he pinged a domino at Rusty, which hit off Rusty's chest and landed in his lap. Pete then burst out laughing and ran out the pub door shouting, "See you for dominoes tomorrow!"

Rusty shouted, "Ya cheeky bugger! Naw you cudny," and he got up and chased after Pete down the street. Bert and Jim were ending themselves laughing and so were most of the men in the pub.

I took a round of drinks over for Bert, Rusty and Jim and I sat down next to Bert for a few minutes.

Rusty walked back into the pub after about 5 mins out of breath after chasing Pete along the street and Cammy shouted from the bar, "Watch out for flying dominoes everybody, here's Rusty back!"

Everyone burst out laughing again. Rusty just sat down in his chair and shook his head and laughed.

I thought, how funny it was in the pub that situations could go from zero to one-hundred in a few seconds then only minutes later all is forgotten and back to normal.

Bullseye

A Sunday afternoon shift, I was starting at 12 pm today and finishing about 6 pm. I enjoyed this shift, it always went by quickly and there was always a good mix of people through the door.

The thinking of a lot of the men that came through the door on a Sunday afternoon was to have a few pints then get back home for their Sunday dinners. This rarely went to plan and guaranteed from around 4.30pm the pub phone would start ringing, it would be the wives of the men who had promised to be home on time for dinner.

I would answer and each time, whether it be Cammy's, Ian's, Pete's or Alec's wife they would all say, "Tell her I've just left."

I would always say, "Tell her yourself, I'm no telling lies for you," and hand them the phone.

It wasn't long before the guys would get wise to the dreaded Sunday phone calls and start answering the pub phone themselves. Cammy and Ian both particularly enjoyed doing this, they would answer and pretend to be a range of different people. Cammy's favourite was to answer in a feminine voice and say, "Hello, sex hotline." Then presumably whoever was on the other end of the phone would hang up.

Ian would answer the phone and start speaking in an Indian accent and pretend to work in a call centre.

Just a daft carry on, very entertaining at the bar, but maybe not so much for whose ever wife was on the phone.

They were fooling no-one though, their wives knew exactly what they were up to.

Cammy and Ian were brother's in law, both their families lived in the village and they were all quite close. They spent a lot of time together and even holidayed abroad together during the summer months. Ian was a small man with fair colouring, he had a quiet confident way about him, compared to Cammy who was big and burly and full of life, Cammy still had a boyish mischievousness to him. Both of them were in their mid-fifties and they got on well with everyone. Sunday afternoon was also when the local darts team would practise. For safety reasons they were only allowed to play darts until 6 pm before they consumed too much alcohol and became a hazard.

So, before I finished my shift I would collect in all the darts before I went home.

Cammy and Ian were both in the darts team along with Shug, Alec and Watty who were all regulars in the Stagger Inn. I have no idea how they ever managed to compete in any competitions as most of them were either hungover or drunk every time they practised. The dartboard hung in a corner of the pub that was out of the way of any route that punters might take to the bar. So that no-one accidentally walked in front of it when someone was taking a shot.

The darts team started practising at about 2 pm and I was happily tending to my customers. Bert and Rusty were in and Sleepy Joe had just arrived with Jock. Jock walked up to the bar and said, "Hiya Kirsty hen, can I get a wee dish of water for Shamus." Shamus was Jock's dog, he was a lovely wee dog. He was a cross between a Jack Russel and a Terrier, he was light brown and wore a wee red collar with his name on it.

I said, "Aye Jock, nae bother. Where is he?"

Jock said, "I've tied him up outside until I saw how busy it was in here."

I said, "Aw, go and bring him in, he'll be nae bother."

Jock said, "Okay hen, thanks. I'll go and get him."

Jock brought Shamus in and joined Sleepy Joe at a table. I took over a dish of water for Shamus and patted him on the head while he took a drink, then I asked Jock and Sleepy Joe what they were having to drink and said I would bring it over.

Sleepy Joe as you can guess is named so as he keeps falling asleep wherever he goes. I've witnessed him fall asleep in the pub about three times I think, one time he was standing up, leaning against the bar and fell asleep. Jock once told me that he was in Joe's car with him on their way home from work one day and Joe fell asleep at the wheel! Jock said, he shouted and shook Joe awake and Joe said, "Christ, I thought you were driving, Jock!"

Jock said, he couldn't believe it, how could he forget he was driving the car. So, Sleepy Joe was well named.

I took Jock and Sleepy Joe's drinks over to them and saw that Shamus had settled himself under their table. The pub was getting busy and the darts team were all on good form. Cammy said, "Kirsty, will you remind me when it's 4.30 pm. I'm definitely going home for my dinner tonight, it's roast beef."

I said, "Aye, nae bother Cammy. You say that every week though."

Cammy said, "Aye, but I mean it this week."

I said, "You say that every week as well," as I laughed and shook my head at him.

Then Watty said, "If you don't go home for your roast beef dinner then I'm going hame to yours to have it."

Cammy was now busy tormenting Ian pretending to lift him up to take his shot and asking him if he needed a stool to stand on. Ian just said, "Shut up you, ya clown."

It was around 4.30 pm and right on cue, the phone rang. The boys playing darts were too busy to notice, so I

18

answered it, it was Cammy's wife Kate. She said, "Hiya, is that you Kirsty?"

I said, "Aye, it is. Hiya Kate."

She said, "Is my Cammy still there?"

I said, "He is but he told me he's going home for his roast beef dinner, wait a minute and I'll shout to him."

I shouted across the pub, "Cammy, it's Kate."

Cammy shouted back, "Tell her I'm throwing my last dart then I'm heading."

Then Ian and Watty started shouting, "What about ours Kate?", "Aye, we're aw coming to yours for roast beef Kate."

I said to Kate, "Did you hear that?"

She said, "Aye, what they aw like eh? Right, thanks hen, cheerio."

So, the darts team were all throwing their last round and a few more of the men had started to talk about dinner and were thinking about heading home. I watched Cammy stand up to the mark ready to throw his last dart when someone walked past Jock and Sleepy Joe's table and stood on Shamus' tail.

Shamus let out a yowl, I about jumped out my skin. I had forgotten he was there.

Cammy also jumped out of his skin and spun around just as he was throwing his dart to see what the noise was but he let go of the dart. It all happened so quickly, the next thing I knew I was looking at Watty with a dart hanging out of his forehead!

Watty didn't have a clue what had happened until he saw everyone staring at him with horrified looks on their faces. He reached up to his forehead and felt the dart sticking out of it. He said, "Fucking hell!" as he pulled the dart from his forehead.

Cammy ran over to him and helped him sit down and I went and got the first aid kit.

Watty wasn't badly injured, he just had a perfectly pierced hole right in the middle of his forehead, it didn't even bleed much when he pulled out the dart.

I don't know who was more relieved, Watty or Cammy. I checked Watty's wound and cleaned it with a sterile wipe for him.

Cammy had managed to hit Watty smack bang in the middle of his forehead, he couldn't have done it if he'd tried.

After I cleaned Watty's pierced head I said, "I don't think you should walk home Watty, is there someone I can phone for you?"

He said, "My Carol's no back for another hour, I'll be fine though."

Cammy said, "I'll get Kate to come for us. In fact, will you phone her Kirsty cause she'll never believe me if I phone her and tell her what's happened?"

I said, "Aye, of course," and went back behind the bar to phone Kate.

Cammy was right, Kate couldn't believe it when I told her what had just happened but said she was on her way.

The guys then started laughing about it, saying things like, "Christ sake Watty, what were you thinking, distracting Cammy with your forehead!" and "Aye, I saw you jumping in front of that dart Watty. Was it so Cammy would take you hame for a roast beef diner?"

Watty seemed unphased by the incident and said, "Aye, I could fair go a roast beef dinner," while the rest of the darts team took great pleasure at Watty's misfortune. I think Watty would have had to have lost an eye before he got any sympathy from this lot.

The ribbing continued, Alec shouted, "Here Watty, see if you can catch this dart wi yer heid!" as he pretended to throw another dart at him."

Watty took all the tormenting well and just sat and laughed.

It was then I said, "Okay guys, I think we'll give the darts a rest now eh?" as I collected in the darts from the team.

Just then Kate arrived to take Cammy and Watty home, she said, "Right you two, come on, let's go," like she was picking up two naughty school children, which was exactly what they were like.

I sometimes think that the guys in the pub need more supervision than children at school do.

Gies a Song

Every second Friday of the month Big Andy came to the Stagger Inn to set up and host a karaoke night. All the regulars liked Andy and enjoyed the karaoke nights. We had quite a few good singers amongst our regulars, Pete, Shug, Sleepy Joe and Cammy usually gave us a song or two.

They all had their favourite songs that they would sing each time and God help anyone who sang someone else's song! I remember one time Pete started singing, 'My Way' by Frank Sinatra, which was Shug's song and Shug went off his heid. He ran up to Pete and grabbed the microphone out of his hand and started hitting him with it, then he wouldn't give it back until Big Andy changed the song. Everyone was rolling about laughing at them. Pete probably did it on purpose to wind Shug up.

Big Andy was a good singer himself and always sang a few songs to get the night started. He was a tall, broad man with fair, greying hair. If you didn't know him you might think he was quite an imposing figure, not the kinda guy you would like to bump into on a dark night but he was a gentle giant. He had a lovely tone to his voice, so it was not surprising that he was a good singer. I always thought he would have been a good storyteller.

So, I started my Friday night shift and the punters were through the door sharp, looking forward to karaoke night. Shug was always in the pub early on the karaoke nights, he fancied himself as a bit of an entertainer. According to some of the men in the pub, he fancied himself as a lot of things. Shug was always very presentable, he always liked to look good. As he said,

"You never know, I might meet the woman of my dreams today."

He always wore jeans and a smart shirt with different brogues to match. Shug had loads of braw brogues, plain black ones, tan and cream, plain brown and black and grey ones. What can I say, the man liked his shoes. Shug was a likeable guy, very sociable, a right people person. Unfortunately, he had been unlucky in love. He had been married and divorced twice but was always talking about his latest girlfriend or acquaintance he'd met online.

The guys in the pub had various nicknames for Shug, The Big Romancer, Casanova and Mr Luvva Luvva.

Big Andy was setting up his equipment when Shug walked in. Shug said, "Hello Big Andy my friend, hope you've got my tunes ready for tonight?" in his usual cheery way.

Big Andy said, "Don't you worry pal, you're on my list."

Shug walked up to the bar and said, "Well Kirsty darlin, are ye ready for me to serenade you tonight?"

I laughed and said, "You know me Shug, I love a song."

I poured Shug his pint and chatted at the bar with him while the pub started to fill up. Cammy, Ian, Sleepy Joe, Jock, Watty, Pete, Alec, Bert and Rusty were all in for the karaoke.

The karaoke nights also attracted the ladies, much to Shug's delight. We didn't get many female customers, occasionally on a Saturday, some of the wives would come and have a drink with their men, so it was a refreshing change.

Next in through the door bursts Jackie and four of her pals. Cammy said, "Aw Naw."

I smiled as the girls made their way to the bar. Jackie was Cammy's sister, she was an absolute riot, I loved her. She looked quite like Cammy, same dark hair and blue eyes with a personality even larger than Cammy's. I started to serve the girls their drinks at the bar, who I could tell had already all had a few. Meanwhile Jackie walked over to where Cammy was sitting and grabbed Cammy, put him in a headlock and started kissing him saying, "What's happening my brother, aw you'll be glad to see us eh?"

Cammy tried to struggle free from her grip and said, "Get aff me Jackie, ya bam!" while the other guys laughed at her.

I thought, this is going to be a great laugh tonight. Jackie and her pals could give any one of the men in here a run for their money.

The girls got their drinks and plonked themselves down next to Cammy's table, then I heard Big Andy's voice over the microphone. He said, "Okay everybody, are we ready to start? I'm going to give you a song first then I'll get you all up."

Big Andy sang, 'Crazy Little thing called Love' by Queen. The girls were all singing and clapping along. Everyone who wanted to sing put their name on a piece of paper with the song they wanted to sing and gave it to Big Andy.

Next person up was Pete, he sang 'Hotel California' by The Eagles. He was really good and everyone applauded him when he finished. Everyone was in good spirits, literally! All having a great laugh and banter with each other and enjoy the singing.

Jackie and her pal Jane were dancing around the pub trying to get the older guys to get up and dance with them. Jackie shouted to Sleepy Joe as she danced past

24

him, "Dinny bother falling asleep Joe before I hear you on that karaoke."

The drunker Jackie got the louder she got and when Cammy got up to sing he could hardly be heard over Jackie heckling him. She then got up joined by Jane and Angie and started to dance around Cammy as he sang. I could hardly serve drinks for watching and laughing at them. Being the only sober person in the room I often saw and heard a lot that others didn't notice. Like Shug trying his luck with Jackie's pal Wendy or the tender brotherly sisterly moments between Jackie and Cammy when she wasn't torturing him.

It was just one of those nights that everyone was having a really good time, lots of laughter, it was good to be amongst it.

Big Andy asked for Sleepy Joe, who had now fallen asleep, to sing next. Everyone started to shout at Sleepy Joe and tell him it was his turn on the karaoke and Sleepy Joe woke up with a fright, jumped out of his chair, took the microphone off Big Andy and gave a note-perfect rendition of 'Beautiful Noise' by Neil Diamond. I couldn't believe it, he didn't look like he was going to able to sing a note, drunk and had just been shaken out of sleep but he was brilliant.

It was Jackie's turn to sing next on the karaoke and out she strutted in her skinny jeans and high heels to Big Andy, who handed her the microphone.

Jackie certainly put on a performance, she pranced all around the bar, or as far as the mic lead would let her and sang 'Man I feel like a Woman' by Shania Twain. She was really funny, she sang the chorus in an overly exaggerated Scottish accent which sounded more like, "Man I feel like a Wuman!" She had the whole pub in hysterics at her.

During the instrumental part of her song, she stood in front of the karaoke and started swinging the microphone around by the lead in time to the music but she didn't notice Shug who was now parallel with her walking back to his seat from the bar and she whacked Shug right on the side of his head with the microphone. She nearly took Shug off his feet, he didn't see it coming and he stumbled into Bert and Rusty's table, he nearly landed on Bert's knee.

I gasped, it was so funny. Bert helped Shug back onto his feet and Jackie just continued her song as if nothing had happened.

Cammy shouted, "Fuck sake Jackie, you nearly took the man oot," as Shug went back to his seat rubbing the side of his head which had a big red mark on it.

Jackie's little mishap seemed to work in Shug's favour as it gave him the sympathy vote with Wendy, who now seemed very concerned if Shug was okay.

When Jackie finished her song, she shouted down the microphone to Shug, "Aw, you'll be awrite Shug, there's Wendy will kiss it better for you."

The singing continued and everyone thoroughly enjoyed themselves, I could hardly get everyone out the door at the end of the night, no-one was for leaving.

As I cleaned up that night and got ready to close, I thought about Shug getting whacked in the head with the microphone, I couldn't get the image out of my head, it was so funny.

I imagined Shug wouldn't be the only one waking up tomorrow with a sore head.

A Loose Moose!

Monday night was the graveyard shift, it was always quiet and I would spend most of it watching TV or listening to the radio. Nothing very exciting ever happened on a Monday night but it was nice to be able to sit and talk to whoever was in.

One Monday night I sat and talked to Alec about music for hours.

It was about 7 pm and there was only me, Watty, Alec and Jim in the pub. We had the TV on in the background and we were all sitting around a table, I had put the kettle on and was having a cup of tea.

Jim took out his pipe and tobacco tin from his pocket and was getting ready to fill it. I said, "Let me see your pipe, Jim."

He was one of the few men that I knew that still smoked a pipe.

Jim handed me his pipe, he said he'd had it for years and that he had been bought new ones as gifts but didn't like them the same.

It was beautifully made, excellent craftsmanship that you don't see so much nowadays. Jim's pipe was so well carved and it had his initials on it. I could see it had been well looked after and Jim kept it in a green, felt lined leather case.

Jim had been widowed about two years ago and came into the Stagger Inn daily, it's become part of his routine, something to fill his day a bit.

Jim was a tall man with broad shoulders, he still looked fit and well for 73-years-old. He had served in the navy when he was a young man and often told me of his adventures, it had taken him to some amazing places.

After admiring Jim's pipe, I handed him it back and noticed it was already getting dark outside, so I stood up and walked over to the windows and started to close the blinds.

The phone rang behind the bar and Watty got up to answer it as he could see I was at the opposite end of the pub. Watty said, "It's Shug, he's in the chippy and he's phoning to see if we want anything."

Alec said, "Aye, I could go a chippy, I'll take a fish supper."

Watty said, "What about you Jim?"

Jim said, "Aye, I'll take black pudding supper, son."

I said, "Can I get a bag of chips please with brown sauce." I loved chip shop brown sauce.

Watty relayed our order to Shug and asked for a fish supper for himself then he came back and sat at our table. We were all cosied in, blinds shut and heating on waiting on Shug to arrive with our chippy order.

Shug arrived after about 20 mins, he walked into the pub with the chippy order zipped up inside his jacket, so it looked like he had a big fat belly.

He unzipped his coat and took the bundle that was our food out from his jacket and sat it on the bar.

He said, "Good, it's still braw and warm," as he laid it out on the bar and opened all the wrappers to see which was which. Then he started to serve us all like a waiter in a restaurant, he gave Jim his black pudding supper and said, "Black pudding for you Sir," then "Chips wi broon sauce for the lady," as he laid it in front of me. Then he said, "And fish suppers for me, Alec and Watty."

We all thanked Shug. Jim said, "Yer a guid lad Shug, so ye are, cheers son."

Shug said, "Nae bother everybody, eat it while it's hot." We were are tucking into our food, I could feel the smell of vinegar tingling my nose when Watty said, "Can you mind when you used to get your fish supper wrapped up in the days before newspaper? I used to like that, you could get a wee read while you ate your fish and chips."

I said, "Did it not used to get ink all over your chips?"

Watty said, "Naw, no that I can mind anyway."

Alec finished his fish and leaned over to Jim's supper and said, "Gies a bit of that black pudding Jim," as he reached over and tried to take a bit. Jim smacked his hand away and said, "Get yer bloody fingers out my black pudding. If you wanted black pudding you should have ordered it."

Alec said, "Aw come on Jim, dinny be miserable, I only want tae taste it."

Jim said, "Och awrite, here's a wee bit," and he passed it over to Alec.

Alec was one of those guys who was easy to be around, he wasn't overly noticeable in a crowd or when the pub was busy but I really enjoyed talking to him.

He should have been a counsellor or therapist because he gave off a relaxed vibe that made you comfortable around him and want to talk to him. He lived quite near Jim and he often walked Jim home and made sure he got in alright.

Alec was about 52-years-old, he was tall and slim, had light brown hair and wore dark-framed glasses. I noticed he took them off when he was eating his fish supper as they had started to steam up.

I finished eating my chips and said, "I'll get you all another drink in a minute, I'm ready to burst," as I sat back in my chair and relaxed.

As I leaned back in my chair, out of the corner of my eye I thought I saw something move on the carpet. You know that way you catch a flash of something and you're not sure if you saw something or not.

Watty noticed me straining my eyes and said, "What is it?"

I said, I thought I saw something moving on the carpet over there and I pointed to the spot.

The carpet was brown and beige and had a Fleur de Lis pattern on it. If you looked at it for too long it just boggled your eyes.

Alec put his glasses back on and took and look and said, "Cani see anything Kirsty."

Just at that Watty shouted, "There!" and pointed at a little mouse running across the carpet to the other side of the pub.

I said, "Quick! We'll need to catch it."

Watty and Alec jumped out of their seats and started chasing after the wee mouse trying to catch it. They were bashing into tables and knocking over chairs, they were probably terrifying the poor mouse.

Shug shouted, "See if you can chase it out the door," as he ran over to the door and held it open.

Jim was sitting in his chair with his arms folded chuckling away to himself at how hilarious Alec, Watty and Shug all looked trying to catch a mouse. Alec even fell over Watty at one point during the chase.

Alec shouted, "Aye, just you sit there and laugh Jim."

Jim said, "Pair wee moose, it's just in for a heat."

The calamity continued and there were lots of, "Where is it noo?", "Oh, I nearly had it there" and "Bloody missed it again."

Alec, Watty and Shug were now jumping all over and between the tables and chairs trying to catch this mouse.

I went behind the bar and came back with a box of crisps, which I emptied all the crisps out of and threw the box to Alec and said, "Here, put this over it."

I wasn't afraid of mice but I didn't particularly want this mouse making a wee home for itself and all its friends at The Stagger Inn.

Alec and Shug continued their pursuit of the mouse then Watty said, "I'm bloody knackered," and he sat down on a chair to catch his breath.

Jim laughed and said, "You look like a bunch of nutters. Throwing a box about at a mouse. I've never seen the like."

Jim was right, they looked hilarious, it was like something out of a 'Carry On' film.

Shug had now started laughing as well at the ridiculousness of the situation and lay down on the carpet, still laughing and trying to catch his breath.

Alec was still jumping about the pub with the empty crisp box trying to catch the mouse when Jock walked into the pub. Jock stood in the doorway and looked at us all, trying to figure out what was going on. I can't even imagine what we all must have looked like.

Jim and I were killing ourselves laughing at the table, Shug was lying on the floor laughing, Watty was still hanging over a table, there were tables and chairs knocked over all around the pub, packets of cheese and onion crisps scattered all over the floor and Alec was standing holding the empty crisp box with a manic look on his face.

Jock said, "Fucking hell, what's going on here?"

Before any of us could respond the mouse ran straight passed Jock's shoes and out the door.

Jock said, "Did ye see that wee moose?"

Jim roared with laughter then said, "Three grown men defeated by a moose. Absolutely brilliant, you cudny make it up."

I still laugh when I think of Watty, Alec and Shug chasing that mouse about and when I remember how much Jim laughed about it.

It was by far the most excitement that there has ever been on the graveyard shift.

Dodgy Dealings

Everybody knows a guy like Dodgy Davie. Davie was an absolute chancer of a man, he was always involved in a scam of some description or trying to flog fake merchandise, which had always conveniently, 'fallen off the back of a lorry.'

I remember one time he sold Pete a fake gold 'Rolex' watch, which turned Pete's wrist green and broke after a week.

Even when he told you something as simple as what he'd had for his dinner, you never could trust if he was telling the truth. You could not believe the Lord's Prayer off him.

I always thought Davie was harmless and that he just liked to exaggerate, but some of the older men in the pub like, Jim or Jock had no time for his nonsense and would tell Davie to, "Beat it!" before he even got a chance to open his mouth. They didn't like his lazy attitude to work or the fact that he conned people into buying things.

Most people in the pub were now wise to Davie's dodgy dealings and would just tell him, no.

Davie was about 36-years-old, always wore a tracksuit and trainers with a matching skip-cap and had hardly worked a day in his life. According to Davie, he was always between jobs. According to Jock, he needed, "a hard fit up his arse."

Jock was still holding a grudge against Davie after the time he bought a bunnet from him and his head broke out in a red itchy rash after wearing it. Davie wouldn't give Jock his money back and Jock has been annoyed about it ever since.

There had also been a story going around a few months back that Davie had been caught trying to steal his own gran's pension book and this added extra fuel to Jock's, fire, Jock just couldn't abide dishonesty.

Davie usually came into the pub on a Saturday afternoon and waited until evening. His thinking was that he would be able to see all the regulars that came in during the day and then those that came in as the evening went on. This would give him optimum opportunity to convince someone to get involved with his next scam or purchase his latest sale of the century. Davie reminded me of a used car salesman, a job which he would have been excellent at.

I was serving behind the bar when Davie walked in one Saturday afternoon. The pub was starting to fill up, Bert and Rusty were in, Jim was sitting at a table reading the paper, Pete was standing at the bar and Cammy, Kate, Watty and Carol were sitting together at table and Jock was sitting at a table, presumably waiting on Sleepy Joe. It was scratch card Saturday for Jock and Sleepy Joe, every week they would take turns to buy four scratch cards, two each and try their luck. They would always wait until they were together before they scratched them. It must have been Jock's turn to buy the scratch cards this week as I noticed he had them laid out on his table waiting for Sleepy Joe.

When Davie walked in, he scanned the room, looking for potential targets as he made his way to the bar then he said, "Awrite Kirsty, what's happening?"

I said, "Nothing much yet Davie, do you want a pint?"

Davie said, "Aye, thanks," as he reached into his pocket and pulled out a ten-pound note and pile of scratch cards.

He saw me noticing the scratch cards and said, "Dinny worry Kirsty, I'm no gonnae bother anyone trying to sell them, promise."

Which made me think, what was he going to do with them then?

As I was pouring his pint I said, "So, do I dare ask what you've been up to?"

Davie said, "Well, I've got a few ideas on the go just now."

Pete piped up from the other end of the bar and said, "What's that then Davie? An idea to see how long you can dodge getting a job?"

Davie said, "Naw, I'm just waiting on the right opportunity," then he took his pint and wandered past Jock's table and over to sit with Cammy's company.

Jock walked up to the bar and said, "What rubbish was he trying to sell the day then?" referring to Davie.

I said, "Oh nothing yet, he's waiting on an opportunity."

Jock said, "An opportunity, he wudny ken an opportunity if came up and bit him on the arse!"

I laughed and said, "Same again?"

Jock said, "Aye hen," as he turned and looked across to Cammy's table.

Then Jock said, "See that yin?" as he gestured towards Davie, "Keep your eye on that yin hen, Ah dinny trust him."

I said, "Don't worry Jock, there's not much that goes on in here that I don't see and he's welcome as long as he's not annoying anyone."

Jock said, "Aye fair enough. Do you know though, I'm a great believer in karma and that laddie will get his comeuppance one day."

I said, "Well, maybe so Jock."

Jock went back to his table with his drinks for him and Sleepy Joe and I walked around the tables and collected some glasses.

I think I was serving Pete at the bar when I saw Davie walk past Jock's table again as if on his way to the bathroom, but as he walked past, he accidentally (on purpose) dropped his scratch cards on to Jock's table. He then very quickly said, "Oh sorry Jock, dropped aw my scratch cards there," as he started to gather them all back into a pile.

Jock shouted angrily, "Aw, wait a minute, four of them were mine, stop mixing them aw up!"

It would appear that this was exactly what Davie had planned to do, then Jock wouldn't know which ones were his and Davie could give him back four of his dodgy ones.

I marched over to them and said, "Right Davie, get they scratch cards lifted and get out. I saw that, you did that on purpose."

Davie tried to protest, "Naw, it was an accident."

Jock said, "My fucking arse, it was an accident. Noo, I dinny ken which cards are mine. Ya sleekit git that ye are, well noo your caught rotten."

I said, "Right Davie, give Jock back his cards."

Davie held out about twelve cards and said, "I dinny ken what yins are his."

Jock and Davie then started to argue about the cards, Jock was trying to take all the cards from Davie, they were never going to sort it out, so I said, "Right, why doesn't Jock get the first pick of any four since it was your fault Davie and you can't tell them apart?"

Davie reluctantly agreed as he now had everyone else in the pub bearing witness to the scratch card dilemma. Just then Sleepy Joe walked in and looked understandably confused to see Jock sitting with Davie and a pile of scratch cards with me playing referee. He said, "What's going on?"

I said, "I'll fill you in, in a minute Joe," as Joe took off his jacket and sat down at the table beside Jock and Davie.

I said, "Right Jock, come on, you pick four."

Jock said, "Awrite, but see once I've picked mine, we're scratching all of them to see who got what."

Jock lifted four scratch cards from the table and that left Davie with eight.

Then Jock said, "Right, start scratching, you first Davie. I want to make sure there's no way you can cheat your way out of this."

Everyone else's eyes in the pub were now fixed on Davie as he scratched his cards with a 50p coin.

The first couple he scratched he got nothing, then he won a pound on the next card, nothing again on the next card, then 50p on the next card, then nothing again for the next two and on his last card, he won five pounds.

Jock had a face like thunder, I could tell he was raging that Davie had won anything from the scratch cards.

I said, "Right Jock, your turn."

Jock lifted the 50p coin and scratched his first card, he got nothing, then the second card, nothing again.

I was starting to feel nervous as the suspense built as Jock scratched his third card, nothing again. Then on to the last card, Jock sighed and scratched the last card. He squinted his eyes then held the card up to his face then he shouted, "I've just won one hundred pounds!"

Sleepy Joe cheered, "Ya beauty!"

I said, "Aw, well done Jock. Let me see your card."

I noticed Davie's face was tripping him as I checked Jock's scratch card.

Then I said, "Wait a minute Jock, you've no won one hundred pounds."

Jock said, "Aw what?"

I said, "Look!" as I showed him the winning card, "It says one thousand pounds!"

Jock jumped up out of his chair and punched the air and shouted, "I cani believe it!"

Then he leaned across the table, lifted Davie's hat off of his head, slapped him across the face with it and said, "That my friend, was fucking karma!" as he laughed and took delight in his win.

Jock threw Davie's hat to him and Davie walked out of the pub muttering to himself as Jock shouted, "Oh, I wonder how many bunnets I could buy for one thousand pounds!"

Jock bought everyone in the pub a drink to celebrate his win with him. It was a fantastic moment to witness, I'd never seen someone win so much money from a scratch card before and it made it all the more sweeter for Jock that he defeated his nemesis, Davie.

I don't think Jock would ever have gotten over it if Davie had won that money.

I was happy to hear the next day that the card was genuine and not one of Davie's fakes as Jock cashed in his winnings and he halved them with Sleepy Joe.

So, Jock was right, eventually dodgy folk do get their comeuppance.

In The Name of Love

I arrived at a busy pub one Saturday evening to start my shift and almost immediately got myself involved in a music debate with Cammy and Pete.

I walked towards the bar, passed the table they were sitting at and Pete shouted, "Kirsty! Bet you can settle this for us."

I stopped at their table and said, "Settle what? What are you two arguing about?"

Cammy said, "Naw, we're no arguing. We're debating who's a better frontman, Mick Jagger or Freddie Mercury?"

I said, "Oh, that's a tough one." I was a big Stones fan but then again there's never been anyone like Freddie Mercury.

I said, "It's got to be Freddie for me."

Pete looked pleased and said, "See, I told ye Cammy, the lassie kens what she's talking about."

I walked away and left them to their debate, I had a look around to see who else was in and I noticed that Watty, Ian and Alec were just finishing a game of darts.

Watty said, "I'll collect the darts in for you Kirsty."

I said, "Aye, nae bother, Watty."

The pub was quite busy and I could tell the punters that had been in a while already by their level of noise. The noise level of most of the punters seemed to ramp up in accordance with the level of intoxication they were at.

Watty walked up to the bar with the darts in his hand and said, "That's them all Kirsty, that'll dae us for tonight."

I took the darts from Watty and I said, "Thanks Watty. Where's Shug? Has he not been in for a practise with you?"

Watty laughed and he said, "Naw, did you no hear? He's away getting himself aw spruced up for a hot date tonight."

Pete overheard Watty and shouted, "Has Shug got another imaginary date?"

The guys started laughing and Watty said, "Aye, he's meeting someone tonight and he's away to one of they salons today to get his eyebrows and a fake tan done."

I said, "Oh, he is not?"

Cammy started laughing and said, "He's a big jessie, imagine sitting in a beauty salon wi aw the wiman. A bet he'll come back with his nails and make-up done tae!"

We all started laughing, I thought, poor Shug. What an effort he was going to in the hope that it would help him in the romance department.

Pete said, "I can just imagine him sitting in there, he'll be in his element chatting up aw the girls."

I said, "Is he coming in here before he goes on his date?"

I hoped so because I was dying to see his make-over. Watty said, "Aye, he'll likely be in for some dutch courage."

I said, "Well if he does, you lot behave, don't be tormenting him before his date, he might be nervous."

They all looked at me as if butter wouldn't melt and Cammy said, "As if we would dae that Kirsty."

I got on with serving and tending to my customers, everyone was getting on fine and having a good time. I looked up at the clock above the door to check the time when the door opened and in walked who I thought was Shug, as I barely recognised him.

I kid you not, my jaw hit the floor. I had to do a double-take, I really wasn't sure it was him at first.

As he walked into the pub and closer to the bar, I actually gasped and put my hand across my mouth to conceal my laughter.

The guys clocked him immediately, it was hard not to because Shugs skin was now dark brown, he looked like he was of Indian descent.

His teeth were huge and bright white, he'd also been to the dentist a few days ago and had veneers done on his four, front top teeth. He had also had his eyebrows shaped into high pointed peaks.

He looked absolutely ridiculous but he thought he looked great, I couldn't take my eyes off him.

It was like someone had painted him with creosote, the fact his skin was so dark made the teeth stand out even more, then the eyebrows gave him the expression of permanent surprise or shock.

I thought, Aw Shug, what have you done.

I think the guys had the same stunned reaction as I did at first but it lasted for only about two seconds then Cammy said, "Naw, I just cani haud it in Shug. What the fuck have you come as?"

The rest of the guys started laughing then the insults began to roll.

Pete said, "Holy fuck! They gnashers would give Freddie Mercury a run for his money."

Alec said, "Naw, mair like Shergar!"

Shug said, "Ah think they look great, braw and white. The tans maybe a wee bit dark."

Watty said, "A wee bit dark! You could start speaking another language and kid on you're a foreigner."

I can't even remember who all said what but Shug was terrorised.

"Looks like you got they teeth fae the joke shop."

"You're that dark you'll disappear in the shadows."

41

"You'll blind the pair lassie or have her eye out wi they teeth!"

"The lassie will think you've had a fright wi they eyebrows, they're just about in your hairline!"

"You look like you've been a volunteer for product testing and they fucked up!"

"I tell you, you'd better wear a big badge wi yer name on it cause your date will no recognise ye."

"Or you could hang a wee sign wi yer name on it fae they teeth!"

The laughing and jibes continued while Shug sat with the guys and had a pint. They were even taking photos of Shug on their phones as a permanent reminder of Shug's new look.

I couldn't stop staring at him, he looked so different, a bit like he was made up to play a part in panto. Poor Shug, I wished he had just gone on his date the way he was.

I felt at any point Shug was going to pull out his teeth and wipe off the tan and say that he was just kidding, that's how ridiculous he looked. I could not believe this was for real and he was seriously going to meet someone looking like that.

Although the guys were being cruel, they weren't wrong, the girl will probably run a mile when she sees him, or she'll think it's some sort of joke.

Shug shook off all the insults that the guys threw and didn't seem put off for his date. He sat for about half an hour then said, "Right, I'm away to meet my date."

Alec said, "Oh wait, I think I've got a bag here for you to put over yer heid Shug."

The guys burst into fits of laughter again as Shug stood up and put his jacket on.

I shouted, "Good luck, Shug," as he left.

I thought, he's going to need more than just luck for this date, he's going to need a miracle.

Not surprisingly, Shugs date didn't go so well that night. The next time I saw Shug, I was pleased to see that he had decided to let his tan fade, let his eyebrows grow back in and have his veneers filed down a bit. Thank goodness, I was delighted to have the old Shug back.

Heart Roasted

I was working one quiet Tuesday evening when Bert walked in. I said, "Oh, hello Bert, nae Rusty the night?' Bert said, "Naw, Kirsty hen. I'm just in for a quick one."

Bert didn't go and sit in his usual seat, he stayed at the bar and as I poured his whiskey I noticed that he had placed a small black and white photograph on the bar beside him.

I gave Bert his whiskey and he raised his glass and said, "Here's to you, Robert son."

Bert looked down at the photograph, I was dying to ask him who Robert was but could see that he was deep in thought.

Bert then looked up and saw me looking at him, I just smiled as I didn't want to pry.

Then Bert said as he slid the photograph across the bar for me to look at, "Look what a fine young lad Robert is here, it's been 41 years since he passed away."

I looked at the photo and indeed, the man in the photo was a handsome young man. I said, "Was he family or a friend of yours Bert?"

Bert said, "He was my boy." Bert then went on to tell me one of the most fascinating stories I've ever heard. Bert had been a coal miner all his days as had many of the men that lived in the village, right up until the pit closed in 1987.

He said that he was working a back shift with his shift partner Tam and his boy Robert, Bert explained that they called what we would now call an apprentice or trainee, his boy in those days.

Robert was Bert's boy and he was responsible for him each shift. Bert said, "I had to show him how things were done ye see."

He went on to say that they had decided to work over-time this night. It was a Saturday night and Bert hadn't been keen to work over-time but Robert pleaded with him to wait on, as over-time was good money on a Saturday night.

Bert told me that Robert had a wife and young family, a boy at 5-years-old and a wee girl at 3-years-old. He still considered Robert a bairn himself at 29-years-old. So, Bert wanted to help Robert earn as much as he could for his wee family so he and Tam stayed on so that Robert could earn the over-time.

Bert said, that he can remember them stopping for their piece time. He said, "I can even mind I swapped one of my ham pieces wi one of Roberts cheese pieces and we had one of each."

They were quite far down the pit and about a 5-10 minute walk away from the nearest connection to get in touch with the pit head.

Bert said that they were expecting an easy enough shift and weren't planning on over-exerting themselves.

Bert went on and said that he distinctively remembers, as they were working away that him, Tam and Robert were having a conversation about Robert's wee boy.

Bert said, "Robert's wee boy's birthday was coming up and he was trying to earn enough money to buy the bairn a train set that he wanted."

Bert said, "That's when I heard the first big creaking sound. I shouted, Shhh! Then we aw heard it again, a big creaking and crumbling noise."

Bert said it was really hard to imagine if you had never been down a pit.

He said, "I looked at Tam and saw the horror in his face then Tam shouted, Move!"

Bert said that he tried to grab hold of Robert's arm but Robert jumped in the opposite direction from Bert and

Tam and within seconds the whole place had come down round about them.

Bert said, "In all my years down the pit, I had never seen a collapse like it."

He said that he and Tam had managed to run and jump clear of the collapse but Robert jumped into it. He said when he and Tam got to their feet they were staring at a huge mound of coal and rubble and they both new that Robert was lying at the bottom of it.

Bert said, "I've never had a feeling like it in my life, I knew Robert was gone, the pair boy had nae chance."

Bert said that he didn't remember all that happened after the collapse, just that he told Tam to run and call for help and that he started digging.

He said, "All I could think about was getting Robert oot of there, I started digging and throwing coal aboot with my bare hands."

Bert said that he continued to dig until he became aware that Tam had returned with a rescue team. He said, "I dinny even ken how long we dug for that night, all I knew was that I wasny going hame until I got Robert oot of there."

Bert said that they eventually found Robert's body, he said, "The pair boy was aw cuts and scrapes and covered in coal stoor. I was heartbroken."

I could now feel the tears starting to roll down my cheeks that I had been trying to hold back. I didn't even care, I was so captivated with what Bert was telling me, I could hardly believe it.

He said that they had completely dug through the mountain of coal that had fallen and that he couldn't believe his eyes at what he saw on the other side.

Bert said, 'It was like looking into a dark abyss, I've never seen anything like it. I looked up as far as my eye could see and I couldn't see the top and I looked down as far as I could see and I couldn't see the bottom. Just a massive chasm."

He said it was like being on a different planet.

Bert said that they carried Robert's body up the pit on a stretcher that night and him and Tam sat with him until Robert's wife had been contacted and then the undertakers arrived.

Bert said that after Robert's body was taken away he thinks he went into shock, he said that he just couldn't process what had happened.

Bert said, "Dae ye ken, I lost a part of myself that night, I never did get over Robert dying like that. Just a young laddie, wi everything tae live for."

Bert wiped a wee tear away from his eye and looked at me and said, "Aw hen, I'm sorry. I didny mean to upset you.'

I said, "No, no. I'm fine," as I wiped my tears away that were now streaming down my face.

What Bert had just shared with me deserved every tear I had to shed.

Bert went on to tell me that the week after Robert's death, he went to visit Robert's wife and took the train set that Robert had been wanting to buy his wee boy for his birthday.

Well that was me away again, I said, "Aw Bert, that is devastating, you'll need to stop, you've got me heart roasted here. Wait the noo till I pour us a drink," and I turned away from Bert and reached up to the bottles on the gantry.

I poured us both a drink and we talked about how he still keeps in touch with Robert's wife and children. He said that over the years he was glad to have still been a small part of their lives. He said he felt proud to be able to tell Robert's children of the man he was and how much Robert loved them. Bert said, "I still felt a great sense of duty towards Robert, I had been responsible for him so I felt I had to make sure his family were okay and didn't struggle."

He said that Robert's children now have children of their own, Robert would have been a grandad. Bert said, "I take a bit of comfort in thinking that he lives on his own children and grandchildren."

Bert's quick drink in memory of Robert that night, turned into a two-hour chat with me and although I was devastated by what he had told me, I felt privileged that Bert had shared it with me.

I never imagined that when Bert walked through the door that night that I was about to hear one of the most emotional and heart-breaking stories that I've ever heard.

For a Guid Cause

A regular occurrence in the Stagger Inn was the raising of money for charitable events.

There was always someone selling raffle tickets, a football card or a sponsorship form going around.

The Stagger Inn was an integral part of a small knit community and the regular's in the pub gave generously to many good causes.

They supported the local boy's football team, raised money for the primary school, gave to the care home and hospice throughout the year and were involved in raising money to help many worthy causes. I remember there was a lot of money raised to replace the church roof that had been damaged one winter.

Over the years I've seen people take part in some wonderful and ridiculous challenges to raise money, like the ice bucket challenge, walking the West Highland Way, lying in a bath of beans for a day, assault courses and loads of sporting competitions.

By far, the most entertaining thing I've ever seen done in the name of charity was when the guys in the darts team dressed up and performed as the Spice Girls.

There had been talk about the darts team doing this for a while and I never actually thought it would happen. It turned out to be one of the most successful nights there has ever been at the Stagger Inn.

It was organised months in advance, the aim was to raise money for a local boy to be flown to America to have life-saving brain surgery.

Cammy and Watty worked with the boy's father, Wullie, who would occasionally come into the pub for a pint with them.

So, this was a cause that meant a lot to the guys in the darts team and they took the organising of this event seriously.

They were well supported by everyone in the village and wider community and received donations from many businesses and companies.

Their fundraising efforts were even covered by the local newspaper which helped to create even more interest and support.

I was surprised to hear how seriously the guys were taking their up and coming performance, they would meet once a week in Cammy's garage to rehearse. The thought of Cammy, Ian, Watty, Alec and Shug all singing and dancing about in Cammy's garage to the Spice Girls was hilarious. It was definitely going to have to be seen to be believed.

I made sure I was working on the night of the much-anticipated performance, there was no way I was going to miss this.

With a bit of help from Big Andy and his sound system, the pub was set up for the darts team rendition of the Spice Girls.

There had been tickets sold and hundreds of pounds in donations received before the event. Everyone lucky enough to get a ticket to the performance was in the pub early, eagerly awaiting the show to start.

It was standing room only at the Stagger Inn that night, the place was jam-packed.

Meanwhile, Cammy, Ian, Watty, Alec and Shug were in the back room of the pub getting on their costumes, they had gone all out on this. They had the right wigs and outfits for each Spice Girl.

Cammy was going to be Ginger Spice, Ian was Baby Spice, Watty was Sporty Spice, Alec was Scary Spice and Shug was Posh Spice.

I can just imagine the antics of them all trying to get into their costumes.

Big Andy started to warm up the crowd, he had the tunes on and had everyone revved up and excited to see the guys.

After a few minutes, Big Andy announced over the microphone, "Okay everybody, I hope you're ready for this. Please give a huge warm welcome to the Spice Girls!"

The side door opened and in strutted the guys, looking amazing in their costumes, wigs and heeled shoes (which they were surprisingly good at walking in.)

The place erupted with roaring, cheering, whistling, laughing and clapping as the guys walked out and stood in front of Big Andy's set up.

I could not believe my eyes, I don't think I quite believed that the guys would go through with it.

Once the crowd had settled slightly Big Andy put on the first song, 'Wannabee' and the guys started to sing and dance to the track.

It was so funny, they were getting right into their characters and everyone was cheering them on.

I stood and watched them in amazement. I thought, this doesn't feel like it's really happening, it was quite surreal.

Next, they sang, 'Stop' and everyone was loving it. It was one of those situations that you couldn't quite believe what you were seeing and you couldn't tear your eyes away.

I just couldn't believe the transformation, they had their outfits bang on. Ian in his wee white Baby Spice dress and blonde wig in pigtails, Cammy with the tight Union Jack dress on and ginger wig, Watty wearing a sporty crop top and jogging bottoms and a wig tied up in a long high pontail, Alec in a leopard print jumpsuit and afro wig and Shug in a bobbed wig, little black dress and heels.

The guys had really outdone themselves.

They continued their performance and sang, 'Spice up your Life' then 'Who do you Think You Are?'

They were dancing around the pub cuddling folk and sitting on folk's knee's as they sang. They were certainly putting on a show.

After the fourth song, Cammy took the microphone and said, "Right everybody, I'm about knackered and my feet are killing me in these shoes."

He kicked the shoes off as everyone laughed.

Then Cammy said, "On a serious note though, I just want to thank you all for supporting us tonight and coming along to see us perform. As you can see, we put a lot of effort into this because we really wanted it to be a success."

He got a massive cheer, everyone was clapping and shouting, "Well done boys." and "Gaun yersel lads."

He continued, "We've been overwhelmed by the how generous everyone has been and I'm delighted to tell you that we've managed to raise 5,560 pounds!"

Everyone in the pub erupted again, Wullie and his wife were in the pub and Wullie got up and shook all the guys' hands, saying, "Thank you so much, this is incredible."

It was incredible and it also became quite an emotional night. Even though the guys looked outrageously funny dressed as the Spice Girls, you could see how much it meant to them for tonight to go well.

After all the congratulating and photo-taking settled down the guys relaxed and enjoyed the rest of their night.

They kept their costumes on throughout the night, except for the shoes, everyone except Shug changed out of their high heeled shoes and into some comfy footwear. Shug chose to strut about in his black stiletto heels all night, which was questioned by many.

Folk in the pub were having a laugh trying on the wigs, someone put the Scary Spice afro wig on Sleepy Joe and took photos of him when he fell asleep in his chair.

Cammy gave Rusty the Ginger Spice wig to put on and said, "Here Rusty, is this what your hair used to look like?"

Rusty laughed and he put the wig on. I thought he looked like someone out of a glam rock band.

The night continued and the drinks and fun flowed, I'm sure that everyone in the pub that night remembers it well.

It was an unforgettable night for so many reasons. For most of it, hilariously funny but there was a great mix of emotions and a sense of unity in the pub that night. It reminded me how well people in a small village come together for a great cause.

Familiar Stranger

I parked my car in the small car park at the side of the pub, which was more like a gravelled area of land and got out of the car ready to open up the Stagger Inn on a very cold Thursday night in November.

I remember it being cold and foggy and not being able to see the street lights as I drove along the main street to the Stagger Inn that evening.

As I pulled up and parked I thought, I can't wait to get in here and get the heating blasted.

When I got out of the car and walked towards the door of the pub I noticed a figure of a man standing leaning against the wall of the pub smoking a roll-up cigarette. As I walked towards him, I said, "It's a cold one tonight eh?"

I could smell the tobacco from his roll up as I walked closer to him, he pinged it on the ground and stamped it out and said, "Aye, sure is lass. I know I'm a bit early but do you mind if I just come in while you set up?"

I said, "Aye, nae bother," as I unlocked the door. It was freezing outside and I wouldn't have seen anyone left standing outside.

I didn't know this man, but he did seem familiar to me, like he reminded me of someone I knew. He was wearing brown cord trousers and had a bright red scarf tucked into his charcoal grey duffel coat and he had grey frizzy hair sticking out from underneath a checked bunnet.

We walked into the pub and I immediately started putting on all the radiator and heaters, I switched on all the lights and went into the cellar and turned on the gas and pumps.

When I returned from the cellar the man was sitting on a stool at the bar rolling another cigarette.

I said, "Okay, it'll heat up in here soon. What can I get you?"

The man said, "A single malt, please lass."

I poured his drink and started to make polite conversation, "So, are you from the village? I've never seen you in here before."

He said, "Aye, born and bred here but I've been away from the village for a while now, I'm just back for a visit. What about yourself lass, are you from here?"

I said, "Aye, I am that. I'm a McCallum."

He said, "The McCallum's. Oh aye, I worked with McCallum's when I was younger. A big family of them in the village eh?"

I said, "Aye, there's loads of us, I've got cousins I've not even met yet."

Then he said, "Are you expecting it to be busy tonight then?"

I said, "I'll probably still get a few of the regulars in even with it being bitter out there."

He said, "It's starting to heat up in here now though, that's better," and he took his red scarf off and laid it on the bar.

I said, "I'm just going to give the tables a wee wipe down."

He said, "Aye, don't mind me, lass."

So, I walked around the pub, wiped the tables and laid out fresh beer mats.

By the time I got around the pub and back behind the bar the man had finished his drink and said, "I'll just go and have my roll-up."

I said, "Nae bother," and I watched him as he walked out of the door to have his roll-up cigarette. I noticed that he had left his scarf sitting on the bar and I thought, he would have been better putting that back on to stand out there in the freezing cold.

Less than 5 mins had passed and I was stocking one of the fridges with bottled beers when I heard the pub door creak open again, I said, "I wondered how long you would last out there, too cold out there tonight eh?"
Then I heard Jim's voice say, "What's that Kirsty hen?"
I was surprised to see it was Jim and Alec who had walked through the door.
I said, "Oh, I thought you were someone else."
Jim and Alec sat down at a table and I walked over and joined them. They were wrapped up like Eskimos, big jackets with hoods, hats, scarfs and gloves, they sat bundled up for a few minutes before they started to de-robe.
I poured Jim and Alec's drinks and brought them over to their table, Jim said, "You've got the place braw and warm for us Kirsty."
I said, "Oh, you wouldn't have been saying that a wee while ago, it was baltic in here when me and that guy first came in. I'm surprised he's managed to stand out there long enough to smoke that roll-up."
Alec said, "What guy?"
I said, "That guy outside, he just went out to have a smoke a few minutes before you came in."
Jim said, "I never seen anybody, did you, Alec?"
Alec said, "Naw, there was naebody outside hen."
I said, "You sure?" and I stood up and walked over to the door and looked outside. I stood in the doorway and looked around, it was still foggy outside and unless someone was standing within 6 ft of you, you wouldn't have seen them. He was nowhere to be seen, so I came back into the pub and closed the door.
I said to Jim and Alec, "He's not there now, he must have gone away home."
Jim said, "Aye, it's no a night for hanging about."

I said, "Oh wait tho, he left his scarf on the bar," and I turned around to retrieve his scarf from the bar but it was gone.

Jim and Alec were now looking rather confused and Alec said, "Aw, come on Kirsty, you're too young to be losing the plot."

I said, "Naw, it was here, he left it right here," as I gestured to the where he had left it on the bar.

I went on, "It was a red scarf and he sat on that barstool, had a single malt and left his scarf there," as I pointed again to the bar and the bar stool.

Then I realised that the glass that he had left on the bar was also gone. I said, "Right you two, are you winding me up, did you move his scarf and tumbler?"

Jim laughed and said, "Naw we're no hen, we never seen a thing."

Alec said, "We're just in, honest Kirsty, we never saw anyone or moved anything."

I started to feel a bit strange and I sat back down with Jim and Alec. Jim said, "Are you feeling alright hen?"

I started to feel lightheaded and slightly unnerved.

I said, "Just before you came in I served and was talking to a man and he went outside for a smoke and left his scarf sitting on the bar."

I told Jim and Alec that he was waiting outside the pub when I arrived and that I let him come in and sit while I was getting organised. I told them that the man had said that he was from here and that he recognised my family name.

I said, "You would have seen him when you walked in, I thought it was him coming back in when you both walked in."

Jim and Alec could see that I was quite unsettled by my mystery visitor as it would now seem like he had vanished into thin air along with his scarf and glass that he had left on the bar.

Jim and Alec could both see how adamant I was that I had seen and spoken to this man. I started to describe the man and I noticed the expression on Jim's face change. He was initially amused at my confusion then he looked stony serious as I described what the man was wearing and what he looked like.

I saw how Jim was looking at me and I said, "What is it?"

Jim said, "Was the man wearing a dark grey duffel coat?"

I said, "Aye, how do you know that? Did you pass him on the way here?"

Alec was now looking as intrigued as I was and Jim said, "I think ah ken who it was. You've just exactly described Bill Mackie."

Alec's eyes widened as he looked at Jim and I said, "Who's Bill Mackie?"

Jim said, "Bill Mackie lived here all his life and one day he went to his work and never came home.

The hairs stand up on the back of my neck and I got goose bumps all over my body, I was so creeped out at what Jim had just said.

Jim said that he was reported missing and the police searched for him for weeks. They never found him and after a while, he was presumed dead. There was a service held for him and a headstone erected in the cemetery.

Jim said, "Aye, it was a right mystery what happened to Bill, folk talked in the village about it for years. It was like he just disappeared. You'll be too young to mind any of this Kirsty."

I started to feel very uneasy and a bit frightened by what Jim was telling me and wonder what or who on earth it was I had just encountered.

I said, "Aw, please don't tell me I've just been talking to a ghost?"

Then Alec started to freak me out and said, "What if it was him and he's no dead at all."

Jim said, "Naw, he would be near 100 years old now."

I couldn't believe we were actually having this conversation or that Jim and Alec didn't seem too vexed about it. I suppose they hadn't seen or spoken to this stranger so didn't feel unsettled about as I did.

I said, "Well he sat and drank a malt whiskey, it'll be the first ghost I've heard of that can drink."

Jim and Alec laughed and we talked about Bill Mackie and all the conspiracy theories surrounding his disappearance that there had been over the years. There had been many theories, that Bill had been murdered, that he was on the run and fled to another country, that he was abducted by aliens and that he won the lottery and buggered off to travel the world.

I did find it very strange that they never found him, dead or alive, I would have thought at some point he would have turned up.

I also couldn't believe that I had possibly been speaking to a ghost, there was no other plausible explanation but I just couldn't get my head around it.

I thought about it all night and I also made Jim and Alec wait with me until finishing time and until I locked up the pub. I was scared that the minute Jim and Alec left, my mystery visitor would return.

Jim and Alec did help to take my mind off my experience and I felt settled by the time we were leaving.

When we left the pub that night, it was still bitterly cold and foggy outside.

I gave Jim and Alec a lift home in my car, after my spooky experience I didn't want to be left with the worry that Jim and Alec might disappear into the fog and never be seen again.

I sat for ages at home thinking if I had really been in the company of Bill Mackie's ghost and I came to the conclusion that if Bill had returned from the grave then I was glad that I was able to show him some hospitality and serve him in his local pub again.

Oh, Christmas Tree

Christmas time is my absolute favourite time of year. I love everything about it, especially when it's time to put up the tree and decorations. In my own house I always get a real tree, the biggest one I can find, so that it touches the ceiling! I love that gorgeous fresh pine smell that a real tree gives off.

I take great pleasure in decorating my tree then admiring it for the weeks to come.

So, at the Stagger Inn I am more than happy when it comes the time to get out the Christmas decorations and put up the tree.

We have an artificial tree at the pub, some artificial trees can look a bit cheap and scabby but this was a nice one. It was about 7 ft tall, quite thick and full and it had little pine cones and berries through it.

I had made a start to the Christmas decorations in the pub when I was working one Tuesday night at the end of November.

It wasn't long before I had the place looking fabulous and festive, with garlands, hanging bauble arrangements, twinkling lights and wreaths. I saved the tree until last and took my time making it just perfect. As I untangled the lights I had a laugh to myself, it always reminded me of my mum and dad and the arguments that they would have over Christmas tree lights! Christmas tree lights always seemed to become a major problem in our household. My dad used to lay them out all over the living room floor and meticulously check every bulb for a fault. Then guaranteed he would either stand on them and smash them or he would give himself an electric shock while he fiddled about with them or the fuse would go on the plug as soon as he got them on the tree and he would freak out and start ripping them back off the tree as he cursed them. I often wondered if other families had so many difficulties with Christmas tree lights.

Luckily I had not inherited these problems with Christmas tree lights from my dad and I had the tree lights untangled and spaced out perfectly on the tree. Next I went on to the baubles and ornaments, this was my favourite part. I took my time doing this and made sure that the baubles and ornaments were perfectly placed, according to size, colour and shape. I would take a step back from the tree every now and again so that I could have a good look at it and make sure it was all coming together just the way I liked it.

Last of all, I put a sparkly silver star at the very top of the tree.

I thought the finished tree looked wonderful and I was going to admire my tree decorating skills for the rest of my shift.

The whole pub just looked so much more welcoming and cosier. Most of the regular's knew of my love for Christmas and how possessive I was about the Christmas tree. They would often tease me and say things like, "Dinny get too close to that tree now or you'll give Kirsty a heart attack," or "Watch you dinny stand still for too long, or Kirsty will decorate you!" They would also try and move baubles around on it and hang their hats on it to annoy me. I would just threaten to not serve them and that usually made them leave the tree alone.

Having the Stagger Inn looking so lovely inside helped to forget how horrendous it usually was outside in December. One minute it could be pouring with rain, then the next minute gale force winds or snow. Sometimes the punters would walk in dressed like they were off to or had just returned from Siberia.

I was working on the Friday night after I had put up the Christmas decorations. It was nice to see all the punter's coming in, getting warm and comfortable and enjoying their new festive surroundings.

The pub had a good atmosphere about it, must have been the Christmas spirit creeping in.

Loads of the regulars were in and a few new people also stopping in for a drink. Cammy, Ian, Watty and Shug were standing at the bar, Jim, Alec, Jock and Sleepy Joe were sitting at a table together (plus Shamus under the table), Pete was doing the rounds and Bert and Rusty were at their usual table joined by Rusty's son, Tommy.

I had never met Tommy before but I could have guessed a mile off that he was Rusty's son. He looked exactly like a younger version of Rusty except Tommy still had his bright ginger hair. He even had the same mannerisms and laugh as his dad, it was an uncanny resemblance.

I was serving Ian at the bar who had now stopped drinking pints and was onto vodka and coke. Ian was one of those guys that it didn't seem to matter how much alcohol he consumed he didn't look drunk, he never looked bleary eyed or slurred his words. For quite a small person he seemed to be able to consume and cope with an extraordinary amount of alcohol in his system. I was having a laugh at the bar with Ian and the guys. Ian was sitting on a bar stool and Cammy was tormenting him saying, "Is that better on that stool so you can hear what's going on up here?" and "Yer sitting there like the Jolly Judge."

Ian never rose to any of Cammy's tormenting, he would occasionally tell him to shut up but that was about it.

The night wore on and everyone continued to enjoy themselves, plenty of chat and laughs going on.

I watched Ian knock back what was left in his glass and he sat it down on the bar in front of him.

I said, "You want another one, Ian?"

He said, "Naw, I'm alright the now Kirsty, I need to go to the loo."

What he did next was one of the funniest things I have ever seen!

Ian jumped down off his stool but he must have misjudged the height of it and started to stumble to the bathroom. Unfortunately, he did not recover his stumble and it had now progressed into a flying nosedive which was headed straight for the Christmas tree!

I watched, horrified from the bar as I realised he was headed straight for my gorgeous tree and there was nothing I could do about it. It almost seemed to be happening in slow motion.

Ian put his hands out in a feeble attempt to try and stop himself but it was hopeless. He went flying straight into the Christmas tree with so much force that he knocked it out of its stand!

He then appeared to wrestle or dance with the Christmas tree for a few seconds before the two of them crashed to the floor and Ian was now buried beneath the tree!

All you could see were his hands sticking out a little bit.

I shrieked, "My Christmas Tree!"

Cammy erupted into laughter, then shouted, "Fucking hell, that was like a scene out of the Gremlins!"

Shug was hanging onto the bar laughing and Pete and Watty were holding each other up. They were in absolute stiches, poorless with laughing.

We were all laughing so much that we could hardly help Ian out from under the Christmas tree.

It was Rusty and Tommy who eventually lifted it off him and help untangle him from the lights and ornaments.

I sat with Bert and continued to laugh at the situation, the whole pub was in hysterics at Ian.

I think what made it so hilarious was that it was totally out of character for Ian to do something like that, he was one of the quiet ones in the group and was usually reliable and sensible.

Bert said, "Aye, it's the quiet ones you've got to watch."

I thought, Ian will never live this down, they guys will never let him forget this.

Once what was left of the Christmas tree was salvaged and propped up in a corner and Ian returned from the bathroom, the slagging began.

Ian sat back up on his stool at the bar with little bits of tree and sparkles still on his head and his clothes and laughed as the guys gave him pelters, "Christmas tree wan - Ian nil.", " All hail Captain Christmas Tree!" , "Ian's got a new job, the tree wrangler!" and "I ken what ye were dain, ye were trying tae climb tae the top of it and sit there like a wee fairy!"

The hilarity continued for most of the night.

I never thought I would say this, but it was worth the Christmas tree being destroyed to have been able to witness one of the funniest things to date I have ever seen.

Afterword

I look back on my time working at the Stagger Inn with the fondest of memories.

Although I no longer work behind the bar, I still stop in from time to time to see all my old friends.

I often think of the fun times I had and of the wonderful memories I have and share with the regulars.

I have yet to find a place that compares to a local pub like the Stagger Inn.

In all the different pubs, bars and clubs I've been in over the years, I found that many of them lacked character and were full of pretentious people who were either too busy looking at themselves or at their phones.

In my opinion there is a lot to be said for a small village local pub; warm, honest, welcoming, down to earth and decent and more importantly, so are the people that frequent them.

Cheers! to all the punters in their locals.

Other titles by this author :-

Say Aye Tae The Frock

The Last Laugh

Being Friends With Johnny Tourette

An Alternative To Wedding Etiquette

In Dreams

Bucket List

9 781839 458491